Student Workbook

by
Charles J. LaRue

AGS Publishing
Circle Pines, MN 55014-1796
800-328-2560

© 2004 AGS Publishing
4201 Woodland Road
Circle Pines, MN 55014-1796
800-328-2560 • www.agsnet.com

AGS Publishing is a trademark and trade name of American Guidance Service, Inc.

Printed in the United States of America

ISBN 0-7854-3615-4

Product Number 93903

13 14 15 16 V036 15 14

Table of Contents

Compare and Contrast

Directions When you compare and contrast, you tell how things or ideas are alike and how they are different. Compare and contrast each pair below.

1. microscope and electron microscope

   A How they are alike

_____

   B How they are different

_____

2. tissues and organs

   A How they are alike

_____

   B How they are different

_____

3. skin cells and muscle cells

   A How they are alike

_____

   B How they are different

_____

4. animals and bacteria

   A How they are alike

_____

   B How they are different

_____

5. plants and animals

   A How they are alike

_____

   B How they are different

_____

Plant and Animal Cells

Directions A Venn diagram shows how two things are alike and different.
The Venn diagram below shows which features animal cells and plant cells have in
common and which ones they do not. Complete the Venn diagram. On the left
side of the diagram, write the cell features that only animal cells have. On the right
side of the diagram, write the cell features that only plant cells have. In the center
of the diagram, write the cell features that both have.

cell membranes	DNA	mitochondria
cell walls	endoplasmic reticulum	nucleus
chloroplasts	golgi bodies	ribosomes
cytoplasm	lysosomes	vacuoles

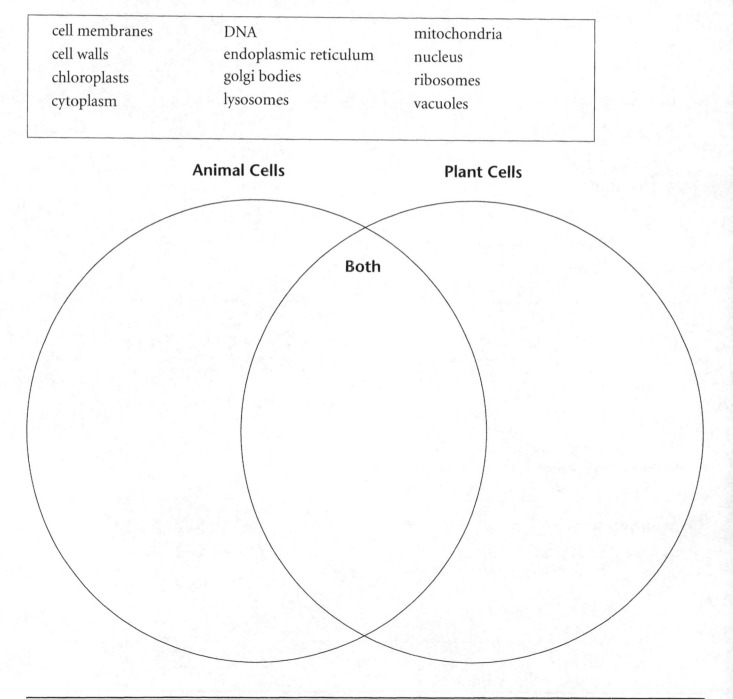

Animal Cells   **Plant Cells**

Both

Chemicals for Life

Directions The following chart shows the chemicals that are important for life.
Complete the chart.

Chemical	Why Is It Important?	Where Is It Found?
1. Water		
2. Carbohydrates		
3. Fats		
4. Proteins		
5. Minerals		
6. Vitamins		

Directions Write your answers on the lines.

7. Use a reference book to find three important vitamins for life. Name some foods they are found in.

_____

_____

8. Use a reference book to find three important minerals for life. Name some foods they are found in.

_____

_____

9. Define amino acids. Tell how they enable proteins to do a wide range of jobs.

_____

_____

10. Compare the role of carbohydrates in plants and in animals.

_____

_____

Vocabulary Review

Directions: Match the terms in Column A with the descriptions in Column B.
Write the letter of the correct answer on the line.

Column A

_____ **1.** microscope

_____ **2.** tissue

_____ **3.** cell

_____ **4.** solution

_____ **5.** amino acid

_____ **6.** bacteria

_____ **7.** vacuole

_____ **8.** lysosome

Column B

A molecules that make up proteins

B a living thing made of only one cell

C an instrument that uses light to magnify things

D a group of similar cells

E a mixture of water and particles

F the basic unit of life

G stores food, water, or waste

H breaks down substances in animal cells

Directions: Write the term that is described. Use the words in the Word Bank.

Word Bank

atom	endoplasmic reticulum	mitochondrion
cell membrane	homeostasis	nucleus
chloroplast		

9. control center of the cell _____

10. system of tubes that transports proteins _____

11. smallest particle of an element _____

12. thin layer surrounding a cell _____

13. captures light energy from the Sun _____

14. uses oxygen to break down food for energy _____

15. the ability of an organism to maintain its internal condition _____

Classifying Information

Scientists organize information by putting it into categories.

Directions Read each sentence. Decide whether each object is living or nonliving. Write L for Living or N for Nonliving. Write both L and N if the sentence could fit either category.

_____ **1.** They carry out all basic life activities.

_____ **2.** They are rocks, soil, water, or gases.

_____ **3.** They are hard enough to cut steel.

_____ **4.** They must make or capture food.

_____ **5.** They do not move around by themselves.

_____ **6.** They are made of cells.

_____ **7.** They do not grow and develop.

_____ **8.** They have properties such as size, shape, and color.

Directions Write the word or words needed to complete each sentence.

9. A complete living thing is called a(n) _____.

10. You can tell if a thing is living or nonliving by observing its
_____.

11. A thing that carries out only one life activity is _____.

12. The simplest organisms are _____.

13. Most organisms have _____ that do specific jobs
to carry out life activities.

Directions Answer each question with a phrase or sentence.

14. What properties are most important to identify nonliving things?

_____

15. What properties are most important to identify living things?

_____

Vocabulary Review

Directions: Match each term in Column A with its meaning in Column B.
Write the correct letter on the line.

Column A		Column B
_____ **1.** cilia	**A**	an organism that absorbs food from another organism and harms it
_____ **2.** moneran	**B**	an organism of many cells that decomposes material to get its food
_____ **3.** protist	**C**	one of the five main groups into which living things are classified
_____ **4.** protozoan	**D**	the study of living things
_____ **5.** kingdom	**E**	hair-like structures that help some one-celled organisms move
_____ **6.** parasite	**F**	an organism that usually is one-celled and has plant-like or animal-like properties
_____ **7.** biology	**G**	an organism that is one-celled and does not have organelles
_____ **8.** flagellum	**H**	whip-like tail that helps some one-celled organisms move
_____ **9.** taxonomy	**I**	the science of classifying organisms according to their similar features
_____**10.** fungus	**J**	a protist that has animal-like qualities

Directions: Unscramble the word or words in parentheses to
complete each sentence below.

11. Fungi release special chemicals on dead plant and animal matter to
_____ them. (mdeosepoc)

12. Large _____ called seaweeds can live in the ocean. (egala)

13. Biologists using the microscope discovered tiny _____.
(smmooicranrgis)

14. Amoebas move by pushing out part of their cell in a _____.
(speduodpo)

15. An individual living thing is called a(n) _____. (somgrain)

16. An _____ lacks one shape because it pushes out parts
of its cell to move itself. (baameo)

17. A quality that describes an object is a(n) _____. (topperry)

18. The system of _____ groups organisms with
similar features. (moxyoant)

19. A euglena is an example of a _____. (aportzoon)

20. The monera kingdom contains only _____. (itrabcea)

Name _____ Date _____ Period _____

Workbook Activity

Chapter 3, Lesson 1

7

The Classification of Animals

Directions Fill in the missing levels of classification.
Then write levels that are used to show scientific name.

kingdom

1. _____

2. _____

order

family

3. _____

4. _____

5. Scientific name = _____ + _____

Directions Write the word or words needed to complete each sentence.

6. Scientists use the science called _____ to classify
   organisms based on how they are _____.

7. The highest level in the classification system is _____.

8. The lowest level in the classification system is _____.

9. As you move from an animal's class to its order, it becomes part of a _____
   group that is _____ closely related.

10. A scientific name belongs to _____ species.

Directions Answer each question with a phrase or sentence.

11. What does the species level represent?

   _____

12. Which animals are more closely related, those in the same order or the same genus?

   _____

13. Why do we use scientific names rather than common names in science?

   _____

14. What mistakes have been made in writing this scientific name: felis concolor.

   _____

15. Why are we unable to say how many kinds of animals there are in the world?

   _____

Biology

Distinguishing Vertebrates

Directions Name the three characteristics that set vertebrates apart from other animals.

1. _____

2. _____

3. _____

Directions Complete the table by writing the letter of the correct description for each group of vertebrates.

Descriptions

A Have dry, scaly skin. Lay eggs with a soft shell.

B Have gills, scales, and a skeleton made of cartilage.

C Have hair and mammary glands.

D Have gills, scales, and a skeleton made of bone.

E Have thin, moist skin. As adults, breathe with lungs or through their skin.

F Have gills and a skeleton made of cartilage. Do not have scales or jaws.

G Have feathers, hollow bones, and a horny beak. Lay eggs with a hard shell.

Features of Vertebrate Groups

Group	Description	Approximate Number of Species
4. Bony fishes		24,000
5. Sharks, rays, and skates		800
6. Lampreys and hagfishes		80
7. Amphibians		4,000
8. Reptiles		7,000
9. Birds		9,000
10. Mammals		4,400

Vocabulary Review

Directions Match each term in Column A with its meaning in Column B.
Write the correct letter on the line.

Column A

_____ **1.** genus

_____ **2.** tentacle

_____ **3.** pupa

_____ **4.** complete metamorphosis

_____ **5.** cartilage

_____ **6.** incomplete metamorphosis

_____ **7.** gill

_____ **8.** vertebrates

_____ **9.** molting

_____ **10.** tube foot

_____ **11.** vertebra

_____ **12.** phylum

_____ **13.** species

_____ **14.** invertebrates

_____ **15.** classify

Column B

A a material in vertebrate skeletons, softer than bone

B breathing structure for vertebrates that live in water

C small tube used by echinoderms for moving

D shedding of external skeleton, characteristic of arthropods

E third stage of complete metamorphosis, stage before adult

F changes in form during development in which earlier stages do not look like the adult

G changes in form during development in which earlier stages look like the adult

H to group things based on their shared characteristics

I the sixth classification level of biology, contains separate species

J arm-like body part of invertebrates, used to catch prey

K a group of organisms that can breed with each other to produce offspring like themselves

L subdivision of a kingdom with the second largest group of organisms

M animals with backbones

N one of the bones or blocks of cartilage that make up a backbone

O animals without backbones

Classifying Plants

Directions Use the clue to complete the word or words below it. Hint: Vowels are missing in the answer blocks.

Two scientists who worked to classify plants

1. | | r | | s | t | | t | l | | |

2. | L | | n | n | | | | s |

Two groups in scientific names of plants

3. | g | | n | | s |

4. | s | p | | c | | | s |

Genus and species of the red maple

5. | | c | | r |

6. | r | | b | r | | m |

One example: a drinking straw

7. | t | | b | |

8. | v | | s | s | | l |

Plant tissue containing tubes; also, an example in a leaf

9. | v | | s | c | | l | | r |

10. | v | | | n |

Well developed parts in vascular plants

11. | s | t | | m | s |

12. | l | | | v | | s |

13. | r | | | t | s |

Plants that do not have tubelike cells

14. | n | | n | v | | s | c | | l | | r |

What plants without tubelike cells must always have nearby

15. | m | | | s | t | | r |

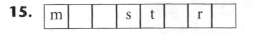

Seed Plants: Terms Review

Directions Complete the following paragraph using the terms below.

angiosperms	monocots	seeds
dicots	parallel	two

Most species of plants are **1.** _____, or flowering plants.

They have flowers that form fruit and **2.** _____. They are

divided into two kinds, **3.** _____ and dicots. Most angiosperms are

4. _____. Dicots have **5.** _____ seed leaves

and their veins are crisscrossed. The veins of monocot leaves are **6.** _____.

Monocots have only one seed leaf.

Directions Complete the following paragraph using the terms below.

cone	ginkgo tree	leaves
conifers	green	paper
fruit	gymnosperms	trees

Seed plants that do not have flowers are called **7.** _____. Their seeds

are not surrounded by a **8.** _____. Instead, they may be produced

inside a **9.** _____. The major group of gymnosperms is

10. _____. They are all **11.** _____

or woody shrubs. Most have **12.** _____ leaves all year. They are a major

source of **13.** _____ and other wood products. Another

example of a gymnosperm is the **14.** _____. It has fan-shaped

15. _____.

Vocabulary Review

Directions Choose a term from Column B that matches the clue in the column A.
Write the letter of that term in the blank.

Column A		**Column B**	
_____ **1.**	has tubelike tissue	**A**	conifer
_____ **2.**	seedless plant, with fronds	**B**	cotyledon
_____ **3.**	dead plant material in topsoil	**C**	seed
_____ **4.**	not a seed, but a ___	**D**	genus
_____ **5.**	spore clusters under fern leaf	**E**	gymnosperm
_____ **6.**	has hard outer coat	**F**	spore
_____ **7.**	name for flowering plant	**G**	dicot
_____ **8.**	fern leaf	**H**	fern
_____ **9.**	container for embryo food	**I**	angiosperm
_____ **10.**	means "naked seed"	**J**	bog
_____ **11.**	two cotyledons	**K**	vascular plant
_____ **12.**	baby plant inside a seed	**L**	humus
_____ **13.**	has cones	**M**	embryo
_____ **14.**	one cotyledon	**N**	sori
_____ **15.**	wet, spongy ground	**O**	monocot
_____ **16.**	first word in scientific plant name	**P**	frond

Directions Write a sentence describing each term.

17. moss

_____

18. vascular tissue

_____

19. nonvascular plant

_____

20. rhizoid

_____

Bacteria

Directions Match the terms in Column A with the descriptions in Column B.
Write the letter of each correct answer on the line.

Column A

_____ **1.** saprophyte

_____ **2.** endospore

_____ **3.** refrigeration

_____ **4.** antibiotic

_____ **5.** tetanus, anthrax

_____ **6.** mutualism

_____ **7.** rod, spiral, sphere

_____ **8.** sour

_____ **9.** toxin

_____ **10.** ammonia

_____ **11.** Monera

_____ **12.** binary fission

_____ **13.** marsh gas

_____ **14.** yogurt

Column B

A kingdom made up of bacteria

B bacterial shapes

C how bacteria reproduce

D any poison produced by bacteria

E dried-up form of bacteria

F drug that helps fight harmful bacteria

G produced by bacteria in swamps

H a food made with helpful bacteria

I any organism that breaks down dead matter

J chemical that some bacteria make from nitrogen

K milk plus harmful bacteria produces this taste

L helpful relationship between two organisms

M keeps bacteria from growing and spoiling food

N specific bacteria that make endospores

Directions Write your answer on the lines.

15. What have you learned about bacteria that surprises you the most?

_____

_____

All About Protists

Directions Write the correct term to complete each sentence. As a check, find each vocabulary term in the puzzle below.

1. Plantlike protists are known as _____.

2. Animal-like protists are known as _____.

3. A(n) _____ is a protozoan that moves by pushing out pseudopods.

4. Algae produce about half of the _____ in the atmosphere.

5. A group of protozoans called _____ cause sleeping sickness.

J	I	H	A	Q	T	F	I	V	S	Q	Q	M	F	T
H	I	K	F	L	A	G	E	L	L	U	M	W	E	R
T	Y	U	I	O	G	A	S	O	O	U	R	G	N	Y
Z	X	C	V	B	N	A	Q	W	E	R	T	Y	U	P
P	R	M	S	D	F	G	E	J	K	L	Z	X	C	A
R	N	Z	Q	S	P	O	R	O	Z	O	A	N	S	N
O	F	C	V	L	L	T	X	M	B	R	O	O	B	O
T	E	O	E	I	U	I	O	P	A	S	D	X	G	S
O	K	K	Z	C	C	E	B	N	M	Q	H	O	R	O
Z	U	N	O	C	A	Q	D	F	G	W	J	X	L	M
O	C	N	B	I	M	E	W	E	T	T	Y	Y	I	E
A	A	N	D	L	G	Y	J	H	L	Z	X	G	V	S
N	M	B	W	I	R	W	Y	U	A	M	O	E	B	A
S	G	D	I	A	T	O	M	C	V	B	N	N	Q	W
E	R	T	Y	U	M	T	M	S	L	Q	S	M	H	J

The Diary of a Protist

Directions Use terms from the Word Bank to complete each sentence.

asexual	chloroplasts	contractile	flagellum	gullet	spin
cell membrane	cilia	eyespot	food vacuoles	osmosis	

I am a one-celled protist, and I am HUNGRY! My **1.** _____ are all empty.

Maybe I can get some of those tasty food particles into my **2.** _____.

I'd like a drink, too. I'll take small sips so that I don't work my **3.** _____

too hard. I drink by the **4.** _____ of liquids across my

5. _____.

As a protist, I spend much of my time looking for food. My neighbor, *Euglena*, has

6. _____, so it can make its own food. Sometimes, though, it whips its

7. _____ back and forth and hunts for food just as I do. Oops! I'm about to

hit that rock. Now my **8.** _____ will shift direction, and I'll

9. _____ around and around. Bzzzzzz!

Gee, I'd love to see where I'm going, but I don't have an **10.** _____

like some other protists. Well, it's time to split in two. This is my way of reproducing. It is called

11. _____ reproduction

Directions Answer the questions.

12. Why do you think the protist said "I'm a one-celled protist"?

_____

13. What kind of protist do you think this is?

_____

14. Give two reasons for your answer in the preceding question.

_____

15. Where do you think this protist might live? Why do you think that?

_____

Fungi

Directions Complete the science terms by writing missing letters.
Use the clues to help you.

1. Kingdom that includes mushrooms, yeast, molds ☐ | u | ☐ | i

2. Tube-like threads in fungi ☐ | y | p | ☐ | a

3. Food-making organelle never found in fungi ☐ | h | ☐ | r | o | ☐ | a | ☐ | t

4. Contains hyphae, may look fuzzy ☐ | ☐ | c | e | l | ☐ | u | ☐

5. Another name for mushrooms c | ☐ | u | ☐ | f | ☐ | g | ☐

6. Fungus that grows easily on stale bread ☐ | o | ☐ | d

7. Bad-smelling fungi that grow on crops ☐ | m | ☐ | t | ☐

8. Mold poison that can cause liver cancer ☐ | f | ☐ | a | ☐ | o | ☐ | ☐ | n

9. Fatal at once if eaten d | ☐ | s | t | ☐ | ☐ | y | ☐ | n | ☐ | ☐ | g | ☐

10. Itchy skin infection caused by fungus ☐ | ☐ | ☐ | ☐ | e | t | ☐ | 's | ☐ | o | ☐ | t

11. Goes into bread dough ☐ | ☐ | a | s | ☐

12. Spore-releasing structures on mushrooms g | i | ☐ | ☐ | s

13. Chemicals that slow mold growth in foods ☐ | r | ☐ | e | ☐ | v | ☐ | t | i | ☐ | s

14. Disease caused by fungus, not worm ☐ | ☐ | n | g | ☐ | ☐ | r | ☐

15. Medical reaction some people have to mold spores a | ☐ | ☐ | e | ☐ | g | ☐

Vocabulary Review

Directions Check each term that can be associated with bacteria.

1. __ chloroplast	**3.** __ endospore	**5.** __ methane
2. __ commensalism	**4.** __ toxin	**6.** __ binary fission

Directions Check each term that can be associated with protists.

7. __ saprophyte	**13.** __ gullet	**19.** __ anal pore
8. __ sporozoan	**14.** __ trypanosome	**20.** __ osmosis
9. __ mycelium	**15.** __ flower	**21.** __ food vacuole
10. __ mushroom	**16.** __ bacteria	**22.** __ hyphae
11. __ contractile vacuole	**17.** __ chloroplast	**23.** __ paramecium
12. __ diatom	**18.** __ cell membrane	**24.** __ eyespot

Directions Check each term that can be associated with fungi.

25. __ aflatoxin	**29.** __ mycorrhiza	**33.** __ mycelium
26. __ hyphae	**30.** __ budding	**34.** __ chloroplast
27. __ mutualism	**31.** __ trypanosome	**35.** __ cyclosporine
28. __ lichen	**32.** __ digestive enzyme	

Animals Feeding

Directions Compare and contrast each pair below. Tell how they are alike and how they are different.

1. filter feeders—fluid feeders

   A How they are alike _____

   _____

   B How they are different _____

   _____

2. herbivore—carnivore

   A How they are alike _____

   _____

   B How they are different _____

   _____

3. gastrovascular cavity—digestive tract

   A How they are alike _____

   _____

   B How they are different _____

   _____

Directions Write the word or words needed to complete each sentence.

4. Filter feeders must live in the _____ and have some way to
   _____ food out of the water.

5. Fluid feeders such as aphids and bees have _____ mouthparts.

Animal Respiratory and Circulatory Systems

Directions Write the word or words needed to complete each sentence.

1. Mammals have a heart with _____ chambers.

2. The _____ receive blood returning to the heart.

3. The _____ pump blood out of the heart.

4. Blood returning to the heart contains _____ to be eliminated.

Directions Label the diagram. Begin with the left atrium. Label the parts of the circulatory system. Draw arrows showing the flow of blood.

10. _____

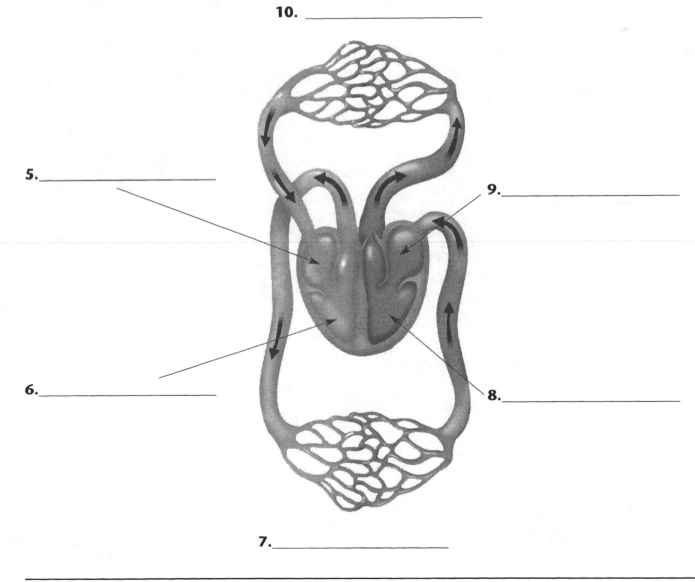

5. _____

9. _____

6. _____

8. _____

7. _____

Water Balance

Directions Write the word or words that correctly complete each sentence.

drink	higher	kidneys	out of	water
gills	into	lower	power	

1. Seawater contains a _____ concentration of water than the fluids in saltwater fish.

2. This means that water wants to move _____ their bodies to make the water concentration equal.

3. These fish _____ seawater to prevent themselves from losing too much water.

4. They excrete excess salt through their _____.

5. Freshwater contains a _____ concentration of water than the fluids in freshwater fish.

6. This means that water tends to move _____ their bodies to make the water concentration equal.

7. Freshwater fish take in _____ at all times through their gills.

8. They get rid of excess water by using their _____ to pump out urine.

9. The urine contains salt, which the fish replaces by using its _____ to absorb salt from the water.

Directions Write a short answer to each question.

10. How do land animals prevent water loss?

_____

Vocabulary Review

Directions Match each term in Column A with its meaning in Column B.
Write the correct letter on the line.

Column A	Column B
_____ **1.** respire	**A** a flatworm cell that collects excess water
_____ **2.** diffusion	**B** an opening through which undigested matter leaves the digestive tract
_____ **3.** flame cell	**C** to take in oxygen and give off carbon dioxide
_____ **4.** cerebrum	**D** a chamber that receives blood returning to the heart
_____ **5.** ventricle	**E** an organ that excretes urine in vertebrates
_____ **6.** kidney	**F** the largest part of vertebrate brain; controls thought, memory, learning, feeling
_____ **7.** anus	**G** a chemical signal released by a nerve cell
_____ **8.** hormone	**H** a part of a bird's digestive tract where food is stored
_____ **9.** atrium	**I** a chamber that pumps blood out of the heart
_____ **10.** crop	**J** a chemical signal produced by glands
_____ **11.** coordinate	**K** to work together; what animal systems do to keep animal alive
_____ **12.** neurotransmitter	**L** the movement of materials from high to low concentration area

Directions Match each term with its description.
Write the letter on the blank beside the term.

13. central nervous system _____   **A** nerves running throughout the body

   peripheral nervous system _____   **B** brain and spinal cord

14. open circulatory system _____   **A** blood makes direct contact with cells

   closed circulatory system _____   **B** blood stays in vessels at all times

15. gastrovascular cavity _____   **A** digestive tube with openings at each end

   digestive tract _____   **B** digestive space with one opening

The Vascular System in Plants

Directions Complete the chart. Identify the plant parts and their functions.
Then answer the question.

Plant Structure	Part	Functions
Root	root tip	**3.**
	vascular tissue	**4.**
	1. xylem	**5.**
	2.	**6.**

Stem	**7.**	**10.**
	8.	**11.**
	9.	**12.**

Leaf	**13.**	**16.**
	14.	**17.**
	15.	**18.**
		19.

20. In what ways are the roots and stems of a plant alike and different?

_____

_____

_____

How Plants Make Food

Directions Complete the crossword puzzle.

Across

1. Green pigment in plants that absorbs light energy

4. Living things need _____.

5. Process in which a plant makes food

9. Simple sugar

10. Organelle where photosynthesis occurs

14. Plants need carbon _____ to make food.

15. Source of energy for photosynthesis

Down

2. A product of photosynthesis

3. Plant parts that contain many chloroplasts

6. What H stands for in H_2O

7. $6CO_2 + 6H_2O + \text{light energy} \rightarrow C_6H_{12}O_6 + 6O_2$ is the _____ for photosynthesis.

8. One product of photosynthesis is one _____ of sugar.

11. A chemical that absorbs certain types of light

12. Oxygen leaves a plant through _____.

13. Photosynthesis provides _____ for plants and people.

How Plants Give Off Oxygen

Directions Use the chart to compare respiration and photosynthesis. For example, in the row "Energy," first tell what happens to energy in respiration. Then tell what happens to energy during photosynthesis.

	Respiration	Photosynthesis
Energy	**1.**	**2.**
Oxygen	**3.**	**4.**
Carbon dioxide	**5.**	**6.**
Water	**7.**	**8.**
Sugars	**9.**	**10.**

Directions Answer each question.

11. Explain the difference between a solid and a gas.

_____

_____

12. Write a sentence using the following words: *stoma, guard cells.*

_____

_____

13. Explain why stomata usually open during the day and close at night.

_____

_____

14. What happens to stomata when the soil and air are dry? How does this help a plant?

_____

_____

15. What effect could destroying rain forests around the world have on other forms of life? To answer, think about what you know about the carbon dioxide–oxygen cycle.

_____

_____

Vocabulary Review

Directions Match the terms in Column A with the descriptions in
Column B. Write the letter of each correct answer on the line.

Column A

_____ **1.** stoma

_____ **2.** phloem

_____ **3.** cellular respiration

_____ **4.** zygote

_____ **5.** ovary

_____ **6.** xylem

_____ **7.** stigma

_____ **8.** pollination

_____ **9.** annual growth ring

_____ **10.** stamen

_____ **11.** photosynthesis

_____ **12.** pollen

_____ **13.** guard cell

_____ **14.** chlorophyll

_____ **15.** germinate

Column B

A ring in a tree trunk formed by layers of wood

B male organ of reproduction in a flower

C vascular tissue in plant that carries food throughout plant

D tiny grains containing sperm

E process in which a plant makes food

F green pigment that absorbs light energy

G vascular tissue that carries water and minerals from roots to stems and leaves

H fertilized cell

I cell that opens and closes stomata

J small opening in a leaf that lets gases in and out

K process in which cells break down food to release energy

L start to grow into a new plant

M lower part of the pistil that contains eggs

N process in which pollen is transferred from stamen to pistil

O upper part of the pistil, on the tip of the style

Digestion

Directions Label the parts of the human digestive system.

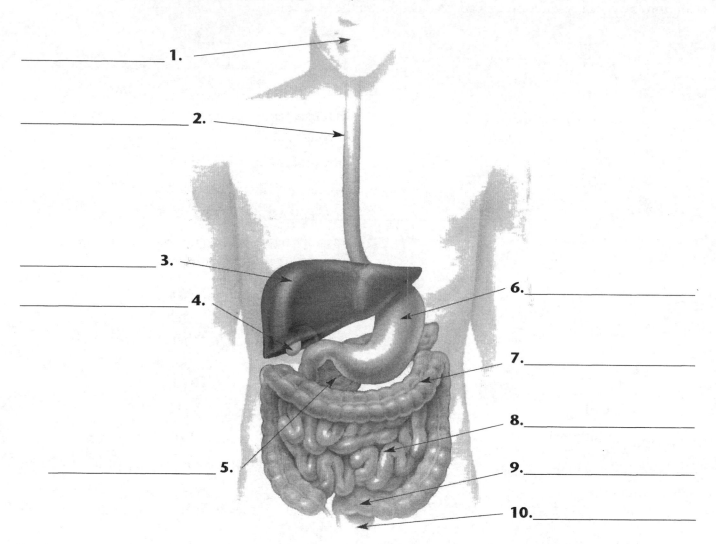

_____ **1.**

_____ **2.**

_____ **3.**

_____ **4.**

_____ **5.**

6. _____

7. _____

8. _____

9. _____

10. _____

Directions Complete the sentences with the correct terms from the diagram.

11. The _____ is a large organ that makes a fluid called bile.

12. Liquid food called chyme enters the _____ from the stomach.

13. The main function of the _____ is to remove water from undigested material.

14. The _____ breaks down food with powerful acids.

15. The _____ is the place where digestion begins.

In Circulation

Directions Find the words from Lesson 2 that best solve the clues. Then write the letters in the blank spaces running across or down.

Across

1. This tiny blood vessel has a wall only one cell thick.

5. The color of blood

6. A blood vessel that carries blood away from the heart

7. The liquid part of blood is called _____.

9. A blood vessel that carries blood to the heart

10. The blood in arteries is _____ in oxygen.

11. A, B, AB, and O each represent a different blood _____.

12. The heart pumps _____ through the body.

15. The organs that fill blood with oxygen

Down

2. Tiny cell pieces that help blood to clot

3. These cells make up almost half of the blood. (3 words)

4. A vein carrying blood _____ a lung is full of oxygen.

8. A protein in plasma that fights disease

13. Without oxygen, cells _____.

14. Capillaries reach every _____ in the body.

Respiration

Directions Label the parts of the human respiratory system below.

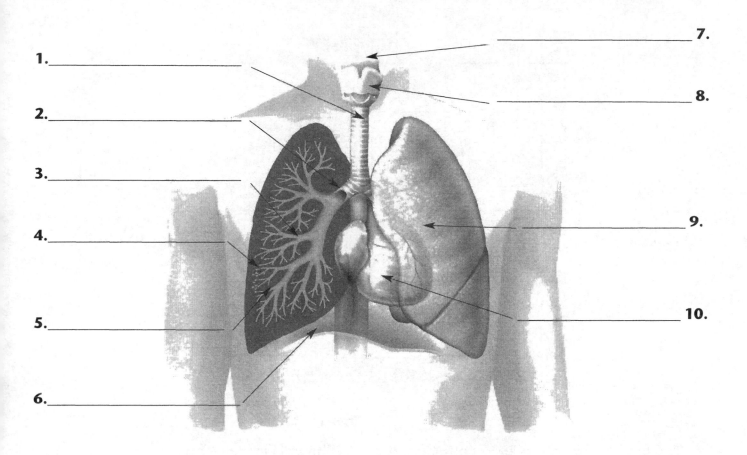

1. _____

2. _____

3. _____

4. _____

5. _____

6. _____

7. _____

8. _____

9. _____

10. _____

Directions Complete the sentences with the correct terms from the diagram.

11. The _____ is a strong muscle that helps you breathe.

12. Air moves from the pharynx through the _____, or voice box.

13. Another name for the _____ is windpipe.

14. The _____ carry air to microscopic air sacs called alveoli.

15. Both air and food share the passageway known as the _____

Excretion

Directions Answer the questions with a word or phrase

1. How many layers of skin do you have? _____

2. Which layer of skin helps keep in heat? _____

3. What substance do your sweat glands release? _____

4. What good effect does perspiration have on a hot day? _____

5. The kidneys are the main organs of what system? _____

6. How many kidneys does the human body have? _____

7. What do the kidneys filter in order to collect waste? _____

8. What tubes carry urine out of the kidneys? _____

9. Where does urine collect? _____

10. What tube carries urine out of the body? _____

Directions Answer each question in one or two complete sentences.

11. How are urine and perspiration alike?

_____

_____

12. Where is the dermis in relation to the epidermis?

_____

_____

13. Why docs your body get rid of wastes?

_____

_____

14. What do water, heat, salt, and nitrogen have in common?

_____

_____

15. How is the waste in your body similar to the waste in your home or community?

_____

_____

The Nervous System

Directions Write the word for each definition or clue.
As a check, find each answer in the puzzle below.

1. The body has a central and a _____ nervous system.   _____

2. Neurons send messages called _____.   _____

3. The gap between neurons   _____

4. A type of action that happens automatically   _____

5. A thick bunch of nerves that runs down the back   _____

6. This important organ consists of three major parts.   _____

7. Another name for a nerve cell   _____

8. The _____ controls the way you think, learn, and remember.   _____

9. Thirty-one pairs of spinal _____ branch off from the spinal cord.   _____

10. The part of the brain that controls balance   _____

I	B	E	W	B	L	I	N	K	I	N	G	L	T
W	Z	E	N	O	B	K	C	A	B	O	H	G	L
N	A	P	E	R	I	P	H	E	R	A	L	O	A
E	L	Q	R	T	E	H	I	K	G	S	H	C	C
U	M	A	V	B	N	A	S	R	S	S	O	E	I
R	E	T	E	K	S	N	G	S	E	M	E	R	M
O	T	E	S	P	A	N	Y	S	Y	F	C	E	E
N	S	P	T	U	H	U	L	P	K	M	L	B	H
O	N	D	B	O	M	U	S	C	L	E	S	E	C
T	I	G	O	G	P	E	Q	T	L	E	I	L	X
G	A	O	P	M	G	T	H	T	A	O	T	L	N
B	R	A	I	N	O	L	Z	X	K	L	L	U	F
S	B	H	O	U	C	E	R	E	B	R	U	M	D
B	R	N	U	D	R	O	C	L	A	N	I	P	S

The Senses of Sight and Hearing

Directions Label the parts of the human eye and ear below, and answer the
question under each figure.

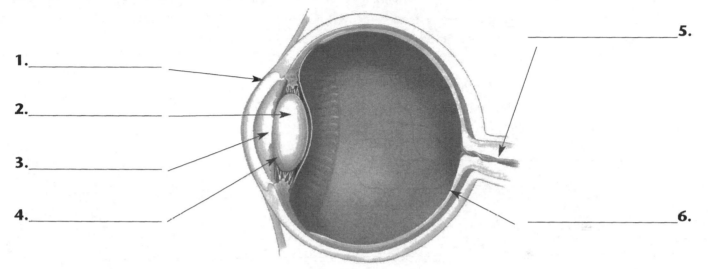

1._____

2._____

3._____

4._____

5. _____

6. _____

7. When you look at the eye, which feature appears colored? _____

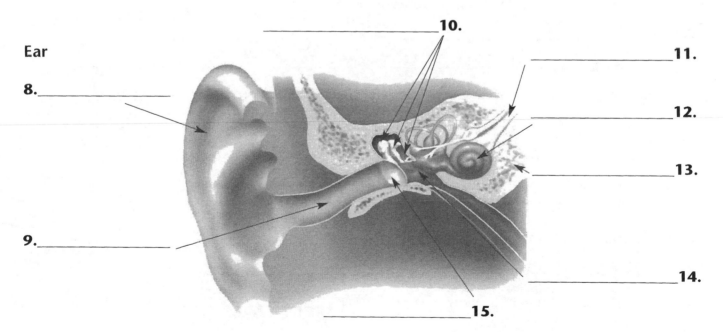

_____ **10.**

Ear

8._____

9._____

11. _____

12. _____

13. _____

14. _____

15. _____

The Endocrine System

Word Bank

adrenal glands	chemical messengers	growth hormone	pancreas
adrenaline	endocrine system	hormones	pituitary gland
bloodstream	feedback loop	insulin	stress

Directions Use the words above to answer the following questions.

What are three important glands in your body?

1. _____ **3.** _____

2. _____

What are the names of three of the hormones these glands secrete?

4. _____ **6.** _____

5. _____

Write the name of a gland and tell what hormone it secretes.

7. The _____ secrete(s) _____.

8. The _____ secrete(s) _____.

9. What hormone can make your heart beat faster and your palms sweat? _____

10. What is the condition it can cause called? _____

Directions Fill in the words from the Word Bank that best complete the following sentences. You'll use some of the same words you used above.

11. The _____ is made up of glands.

12. Glands secrete more than 20 different kinds of _____.

13. Hormones travel through the body by means of the _____.

14. Hormones can be described as _____.

15. Cells send a chemical signal back to the glands in a process known as the

_____.

Vocabulary Review

Directions Match each term in Column A with its meaning in Column B.
Write the correct letter on the line.

Column A	Column B
_____ 1. arteries	**A** protects the body's organs and keeps in heat
_____ 2. voluntary muscles	**B** narrow tubes that carry oxygen to the lungs
_____ 3. excretory system	**C** blood vessels that carry blood away from the heart
_____ 4. fatty layer	**D** a thin tissue that vibrates when sound waves strike it
_____ 5. red marrow	**E** the digestive organ that stores bile
_____ 6. eardrum	**F** muscles you can control
_____ 7. blood pressure	**G** a clear layer of the eye
_____ 8. urine	**H** blood vessels that carry blood to the heart
_____ 9. veins	**I** the force of blood against the walls of blood vessels
_____10. gallbladder	**J** the network of bones in the body
_____11. involuntary muscles	**K** a series of organs that get rid of cell wastes in the form of urine
_____12. skeletal system	**L** the spongy material in bones that makes blood cells
_____13. bronchioles	**M** the liquid part of blood
_____14. plasma	**N** muscles you can't control
_____15. cornea	**O** liquid waste formed in the kidneys

Directions Write the letter of the word that best completes each sentence.

_____16. The _____ is often known as the voice box.

    A bronchus   **B** dermis   **C** pharynx   **D** larynx

_____17. Without the _____, light wouldn't get through to your optic nerve.

    A receptor cell   **B** pupil   **C** diaphragm   **D** osteoporosis

_____18. _____ in your blood fight a battle against disease.

    A antibodies   **B** synapses   **C** capillaries   **D** arteries

_____19. If you get something caught in your _____, you'll have trouble breathing.

    A trachea   **B** epidermis   **C** urethra   **D** cartilage

_____20. Your _____ is like a movie screen in the back of your eye.

    A aorta   **B** rectum   **C** retina   **D** ureter

That's Life

Directions Write the letter of the phrase from the box that completes
each sentence.

A the offspring are unique   **D** only humans can produce humans
B frogs came from mud   **E** a population is more likely to survive change
C living things come from other living things

_____ **1.** Because people believed that living things came from nonliving things,
they thought that ___.

_____ **2.** Because of Redi's experiments, scientist began to learn that ___.

_____ **3.** Because each organism has its own unique DNA, ___

_____ **4.** Because reproduction in most animals involves two parents, ___.

_____ **5.** Because of diversity, ____.

Directions Circle the word or phrase that goes with each meaning clue.

6. living from nonliving   **spontaneous generation** or **reproduction**

7. range of differences   **diversity** or **population**

8. a characteristic   **survival** or **trait**

9. a chemical in a cell   **DNA** or **bacteria**

10. traits that allow survival   **advantages** or **adaptations**

Directions Tell how the items in each pair are related

11. DNA, reproduction

_____

12. eggs, frogs

_____

13. adaptations, resistance to disease

_____

14. traits, DNA

_____

15. spontaneous generation, rotten meat

_____

Reproduction

Directions When you compare and contrast two processes, you tell how they are alike and different. Compare and contrast mitosis and meiosis.

1. MITOSIS and MEIOSIS

   A How are they alike?

_____

_____

_____

_____

_____

_____

   B How are they different?

_____

_____

_____

_____

_____

_____

Directions Write *a* for *advantage* or *d* for *disadvantage* to tell about sexual and asexual reproduction.

Asexual Reproduction

2. ___ can reproduce alone

3. ___ offspring are exact copies

4. ___ can reproduce quickly

Sexual Reproduction

5. ___ must find a mate

6. ___ diversity

7. ___ takes longer to reproduce

Directions Write *asexual*, *sexual*, or *both* to identify the kind of reproduction associated with each word or phrase.

8. nucleus _____

9. exact copy _____

10. two parents _____

11. diversity _____

12. gametes _____

13. one parent _____

14. mitosis _____

15. meiosis _____

Animal Development

Directions Read the sentences. Put the steps of the growth process in order by writing 1, 2, 3, 4, or 5 on the line in front of each sentence.

1. ____ The egg and sperm unite.

____ Cell differentiation occurs.

____ An embryo develops.

____ The zygote divides many times.

____ A zygote is formed.

Directions Unscramble the word in parentheses to complete each sentence.

2. A young insect is called a _____. (hmnyp)

3. A kangaroo is an example of a _____. (aprmasuil)

4. The _____ provides food and oxygen to an embryo. (aceplnta)

5. The _____ protects the developing embryo. (rutuse)

6. Young mammals feed on _____. (ilmk)

7. Most _____ do not lay eggs. (smalamm)

8. A _____ has only one cell but a complete set of chromosomes. (gzyeot)

9. When cells multiply, _____ is copied in each cell. (DAN)

10. A(n) _____ is an early stage of an organism's development. (eyombr)

11. When cells take on different _____, cell differentiation occurs. (bojs)

12. Human embryos get _____ from inside the mother's body. (dofo)

13. A caterpillar changes to a _____ during its metamorphosis. (uppa)

Directions Answer each question with a phrase or sentence.

14. What is gestation time?

_____

_____

15. How do gestation times compare among mammals?

_____

_____

Vocabulary Review

Directions Match each term in Column A with its meaning in Column B.
Write the correct letter on the line.

Column A	Column B
_____ **1.** mitosis	**A** a young insect that looks like the adult
_____ **2.** vagina	**B** an early stage in the development of an organism
_____ **3.** embryo	**C** the process that results in two cells identical to the parent cell
_____ **4.** testosterone	**D** the tube-like canal in the female body through which sperm enter the body
_____ **5.** nymph	**E** male sex hormone
_____ **6.** pregnancy	**F** the development of a fertilized egg into a baby in a female's body

Directions Write a sentence for each pair of words.

7. umbilical cord and placenta

_____

_____

8. internal fertilization and external fertilization

_____

_____

9. estrogen and progesterone

_____

_____

10. prostate gland and semen

_____

_____

The Body Versus Disease

Directions Compare and contrast each pair. Tell how they are alike and how they are different.

	How They Are Alike	How They Are Different
1. phagocyte—lymphocyte		
2. pathogen—antibody		
3. vaccines—sanitation methods		

Directions Use words from the Word Bank to answer the questions.

Word Bank					
cowpox	infectious disease	pathogen	plague	sanitation	virus
immune system	lymphocytes	phagocyte	polio	smallpox	vaccine

4. What is an illness that can pass from one person to another? _____

5. What term is used to describe an infectious disease that spreads quickly and kills many people? _____

6. What is another name for a germ? _____

7. What is a nonliving pathogen? _____

8. What disease disabled or killed many children in the 1900s? _____

9. What white blood cells destroy pathogens? _____

10. What white blood cells makes antibodies? _____

11. What is the body's most important defense against infectious diseases? _____

12. What do doctors give to help the body make antibodies before a pathogen enters the body? _____

13. For what disease was the first vaccine made? _____

14. What pathogen did Edward Jenner use to make the smallpox vaccine? _____

15. What is the practice of keeping things clean to prevent infectious diseases called? _____

Eat Right for Health

Directions List the six kinds of nutrients your body needs.

For Energy   **For Life Activities**

1. _____   5. _____

2. _____   6. _____

3. _____

4. _____

Directions Write the word or words needed to complete each sentence.

7. The types and amounts of foods you eat is called _____.

8. About 70 percent of your body is made up of _____.

9. The body cannot store _____, which fights diseases and is found in citrus fruits, tomatoes, and potatoes.

10. The vitamin found in cabbage, spinach, and soybeans that helps blood clot is

    _____.

11. Calcium and phosphorus are _____ that help build strong bones and teeth.

12. The _____ shows you how to choose the right foods and the right amounts to eat.

13. The _____ a food is on the pyramid, the more it should be eaten.

14. Of all the food groups, You should use less _____ than the other food groups.

15. A serving size of bread is one _____.

Vocabulary Review

Directions Match each term in Column A with its meaning in Column B. Write the correct letter on the line.

Column A	Column B
_____ **1.** immune system	**A** the body's most important defense against infectious disease
_____ **2.** sanitation	**B** something done automatically, or as a matter of course
_____ **3.** drug	**C** a guide for choosing the right foods and servings of food
_____ **4.** plague	**D** material that causes the body to make antibodies against a disease
_____ **5.** vaccine	**E** a unit of measure of the energy contained in food
_____ **6.** Food Guide Pyramid	**F** a substance that acts on the body and changes its functioning
_____ **7.** infectious disease	**G** a quickly spreading, deadly infectious disease
_____ **8.** virus	**H** the practice of keeping things clean to prevent infectious disease
_____ **9.** habit	**I** an illness passed from person to person
_____ **10.** calorie	**J** a pathogen that is not living but takes over the functions of cells

Directions Unscramble the word or words in parentheses to complete each sentence below.

11. _____, such as viruses and bacteria, cause diseases although they are tiny. (staghopen)

12. The two white blood cells that help protect the body are _____ and _____. (chapygoste; chopymeltsy)

13. Antibodies against a disease remain in your body and give it _____ to that disease. (imintumy)

14. Eating enough of the right kinds of foods results in good _____. (untritoin)

15. _____ leads to dangerous and harmful side effects for the body. (grud beasu)

Heredity

Directions Study the Punnett square shown. Read each statement. Answer the questions on the lines provided.

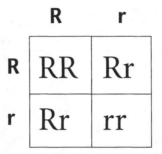

_____ **1.** What genotype do both parents have?

_____ **2.** What letter represents the recessive gene?

_____ **3.** What letter represents the dominant gene?

_____ **4.** What genotypes could an offspring have?

_____ **5.** If r is a recessive gene, which offspring could exhibit the recessive trait?

_____ **6.** If R is dominant over r, what is the chance that an offspring will exhibit the dominant trait?

_____ **7.** Is an offspring more likely to have a genotype Rr or RR? Explain.

_____ **8.** If R is dominant and represents red flowers, which genotypes will have the phenotype for red flowers?

_____ **9.** If R is dominant and represents red flowers, what is the chance that the offspring with the genotype Rr will have white flowers?

_____ **10.** What is the chance that an offspring will not receive a dominant gene?

_____ **11.** Which genotype has a 50 percent chance of being inherited?

_____ **12.** Could these parents have three offspring with the genotype rr? Explain.

Directions Draw a Punnett square for each of the crosses listed below.

13. Rr rr   **14.** YY yy   **15.** Qq Qq

Chromosomes

Directions Complete the chart. Use it to show how each pair of items is alike and different.

	Similarities	Differences
Meiosis/Mitosis	**1.**	**2.**
Gregor Mendel/ Thomas Morgan	**3.**	**4.**
Human sex cells/ Other human cells	**5.**	**6.**
Human egg cells/ Human sperm cells	**7.**	**8.**
Sex-linked traits/ Other traits of an organism	**9.**	**10.**

Directions Define each term.

11. gamete

_____

12. zygote

_____

13. carrier

_____

14. X chromosome

_____

15. Y chromosome

_____

How Heredity Is Studied in Humans

Directions Complete the outline.

Studying Heredity

I. Kinds of Twins

     A. _____

     B. _____

II. Parts of environment that influence a person's characteristics

     A. _____

     B. _____

     C. _____

III. DNA

     A. Definition: _____

     B. Bases

         1. Definition: _____

         2. Names

             a. _____

             b. _____

             c. _____

             d. _____

     C. Replication

         1. Definition: _____

         2. Result: _____

IV. Mutation

     A. Definition: _____

     B. Causes

         1. _____

         2. _____

V. Genetic Diseases

     A. _____

         1. Description: _____

         2. Cause: _____

     B. _____

         1. Description: _____

         2. Cause: _____

     C. _____

         1. Description: _____

         2. Cause: _____

Vocabulary Review

Directions Match the terms in Column A with the descriptions in Column B.
Write the letter of each correct answer on the line.

Column A

_____ 1. applied genetics

_____ 2. sex-linked trait

_____ 3. genotype

_____ 4. environment

_____ 5. factors

_____ 6. base

_____ 7. diabetes

_____ 8. fraternal twins

_____ 9. carrier

_____ 10. cross-pollination

_____ 11. identical twins

_____ 12. dominant gene

_____ 13. self-pollination

_____ 14. gene pool

_____ 15. F^1 generation

_____ 16. genetics

_____ 17. P generation

_____ 18. sex chromosome

_____ 19. inbreeding

_____ 20. genetic disease

Column B

A movement of pollen between male and female sex organs on the same plant

B sexual reproduction between organisms in a small gene pool

C determines the sex of an organism

D Mendel's name for information about traits passed from parents to offspring

E organism that carries a gene but does not show effects of the gene

F twins formed from the same zygote

G molecule found in DNA that codes information

H an organism's surroundings

I genes found within a population

J plants that resulted when Mendel cross-pollinated two different kinds of pure plants

K twins formed from two different zygotes

L caused by a mutated gene

M a genetic disease in which a person has too much sugar in the blood

N determined by an organism's sex chromosomes

O combination of genes for a trait

P movement of pollen between sex organs on different plants

Q process of using knowledge of genetics to affect heredity

R a gene that shows up as a trait in an organism

S the study of heredity

T the pure plants that Mendel produced by self-pollination

Ecology Crossword

Directions Fill in the blank or write the term to complete the puzzle.

Across

1. number of an organism living in a set area

3. that part of earth where organisms can live

5. various populations living in one area

6. living factors in an environment

7. used by organisms to live; water, air, sunlight are examples

8. _____ species have few members left.

13. All organisms ___ with living and nonliving things in their environment.

14. An _____ is all the interactions among the populations of a community and its nonliving parts.

15. process by which a community changes over time

Down

1. something harmful to organisms that is added to an environment

2. ___ rain contains sulfuric or nitric acid.

4. resources Earth cannot replace, such as minerals

6. ecosystem covering large area, for example, an ocean or a desert

9. place an organism lives

10. fuel formed long ago from remains of organisms

11. A ___ community is stable and contains many types of organisms.

12. study of interactions among living and nonliving parts of an environment

Food Chains and Food Webs

Directions Use the terms to complete the paragraph.

decomposers	food webs	second-order consumers
first-order consumers	large	small
food chain	photosynthesis	third-order consumers

Every **1.** _____ begins with a producer. Most producers

make their food by **2.** _____. Producers are eaten by

3. _____. Animals that eat these plant-eaters are called

4. _____. They are eaten by **5.** _____.

The food chain begins with a **6.** _____ number of

producers. It ends with a **7.** _____ number of last-order

consumers. Because few consumers eat only one type of food, food

chains are linked in **8.** _____. Food chains do not end

because **9.** _____ feed on dead animals.

Directions Use the terms to complete the paragraph.

chemical energy	decreases	food chain
consumers	energy	Sun

Plants use **10.** _____ from the Sun to make food. They change light

energy into **11.** _____. Organisms that eat other organisms because

they cannot make their own food are **12.** _____. As organisms eat

each other, energy moves through the **13.** _____. The amount of

energy available **14.** _____ the higher up the food chain you go.

The **15.** _____ continuously provides energy.

Energy Flow in an Ecosystem

Directions Finish each explanation for the flow of energy in a food chain using the words in the box. You'll use some words more than once.

1. Unlimited energy comes from the _____

2. Energy used for _____

3. Energy lost as _____

4. Energy stored in _____

5. Energy used for _____

6. Energy lost as _____

7. Energy stored in _____

| body tissues |
| heat |
| life activities |
| plant tissues |
| Sun |

Directions Answer each question.

8. Who receives the energy stored in first-order consumers?

    _____

9. To which organisms is the most energy available? Why?

    _____

10. To which organisms is the least energy available? Why?

    _____

11. Why is a pyramid shape used to show amounts of energy available at each level of a food chain?

    _____

12. In the energy pyramid featured on page 314, which organism has the least amount of energy available?

    _____

13. Why is there a much bigger population of grasshoppers than of foxes?

    _____

14. Why is the Sun so important to the food chain?

    _____

15. How does energy flow in an ecosystem? Use the words *producers*, *Sun*, and *consumers* in your answer.

    _____

Vocabulary Review

Directions Match each term in Column A with its meaning in Column B.
Write the correct letter on the line.

Column A

_____ **1.** pollution

_____ **2.** biome

_____ **3.** succession

_____ **4.** community

_____ **5.** omnivore

_____ **6.** food web

_____ **7.** consumer

_____ **8.** habitat

_____ **9.** renewable resource

_____ **10.** groundwater

Column B

A a process through which a community changes over time

B the water stored beneath the earth's surface

C an ecosystem covering a huge area

D natural resource that nature replaces

E a set of populations living in the same area

F the place where an organism lives

G a consumer that eats both plants and animals

H a material put into the environment that harms living things

I linked food chains in a community through which energy moves

J an organism that feeds on other organisms; unable to make its own food

Directions Unscramble the word or words in parentheses to complete each
sentence below.

11. A poison gas mixes with rain to form _____, which harms organisms.
(daic anri)

12. Living things are biotic, and nonliving things are _____. (atiiboc)

13. An endangered animal population could become _____ if all its
members die off. (ttexnic)

14. Liquid water _____ from water vapor. (nodnecses)

15. Fossil fuels are examples of _____ resources that cannot be replaced.
(nelannerobew)

Innate Behavior

Direction Write the term from the Word Bank that best completes each sentence.

Word Bank				
behavior	gravitropism	innate	phototropism	species
courtship	habitat	instinct	reflex	stimulus
experience	heredity	nest building	response	territorial

1. A _____ behavior of a peacock is showing off its feathers.

2. When they claim and defend an area, animals are exhibiting _____ behavior.

3. A plant's response to light is called _____.

4. The two main types of _____ are innate and learned.

5. Anything to which an organism reacts is a(n) _____.

6. Behavior is the interaction of experiences and _____.

7. A(n) _____ is where each species live in the ecosystem.

8. A pattern of behavior is called a(n) _____.

9. The roots of a plant growing down is a response to gravity called _____.

10. A(n) _____ is a reaction to a stimulus.

11. Blinking is an example of a(n) _____.

12. _____ by birds is an example of an instinct.

13. Each _____ of birds has its own special song.

14. The way an animal acts is based on its heredity and _____.

15. A(n) _____ does not have to be learned; it is inherited.

Learned Behavior

Directions Match each term with its definition or examples. Write the letter of the correct answer. You will use terms more than once.

     A imprinting
     B observational learning
     C trial-and-error learning
     D conditioning
     E insight

_____ **1.** A person puts a skateboard under a heavy box to move it easily.

_____ **2.** the ability to solve a new problem based on experience

_____ **3.** A salmon finds its way back to the stream in which it hatched.

_____ **4.** A bird learns to sing by listening to other birds sing.

_____ **5.** learning in which an animal connects a behavior with a reward or a punishment

_____ **6.** A dog makes saliva when it hears a bell ring.

_____ **7.** A rat pushes a lever to get food.

_____ **8.** learning in which an animal bonds with the first object it sees

_____ **9.** A dog stays away from a skunk.

_____ **10.** A chimpanzee stacks boxes to reach a banana.

_____ **11.** learning by watching or listening to the behavior of others

_____ **12.** A cat runs into the kitchen when it hears the refrigerator door opening.

_____ **13.** A bear cub learns to catch fish by watching its mother.

_____ **14.** A newly-hatched goose thinks a monkey is its mother.

_____ **15.** learning in which an animal connects one stimulus with another stimulus

Vocabulary Review

Directions Read the clues to complete the puzzle.

Across

1. _____ is sending information.

6. Turning toward it is a plant's _____ to light.

7. Roots grow down because of _____.

11. _____ behavior results from experience.

12. A pattern of innate behavior is called _____.

13. An organism reacts to a _____.

14. People train dogs by _____ and error.

15. A(n) _____ is an automatic response.

Down

1. A(n) _____ is a way of communicating.

2. Animals engage in courtship behavior to attract a(n) _____.

3. An innate behavior is one that is _____.

4. _____ behavior claims and defends an area.

5. Learning by watching others is _____ learning.

8. A(n) _____ behavior is present at birth.

9. _____ is the way an organism acts.

10. _____ is the ability to solve a new problem based on experience.

Changes in a Population

Directions Complete each sentence. Use the words from the box.

evolution	mutations	traits
lethal	populations	

1. The diversity of organisms found on Earth today is a result of the process called
_____.

2. Evolution does not occur in individuals. It occurs in
_____ of organisms over time.

3. Evolution works through _____ that change an
organism's gametes.

4. These changes are passed on to offspring and affect the
_____ of future generations.

5. If offspring inherit a _____ mutation, they die.
Therefore, such mutations are not passed on.

Directions List five ways in which one species may break into two groups and
evolve into two different species.

6. _____

7. _____

8. _____

9. _____

10. _____

Fossils Crossword

Directions Fill in the blank or write the term to complete the puzzle.

Across

2. type of minerals used to date fossils

6. material studied to trace changes in genes over time

7. The _____ scale chart divides earth's history into time periods.

11. reptile-like trait of *Archaeopteryx*

12. scientist who studies fossils to understand life in the past

13. Some _____ evolved into amphibians, according to the fossil record.

14. bird-like trait of *Archaeopteryx*

15. Scientist Mary _____ found DNA in dinosaur bones.

Down

2. result of major environment changes on earth

3. modern horse descended from Pliohippus.

4. time required for one-half of a radioactive element sample to decay

5. The _____ record is the history of life on earth, as found in preserved remains or organisms.

8. Era, period, and epoch are _____ in the geologic time scale.

9. bits of rock settling in layers

10. the space inside a rock left when remains of an organism decay

Darwin's Theory of Evolution

Directions Use a word or phrase from the box to complete the paragraph.

fossils	modification	scientific theories
hypotheses	natural selection	similar

Charles Darwin traveled and studied **1.** _____

that formed in different times. Older and newer rock layers held fossils that were

2. _____ but somewhat changed over time. He observed plants

and animals of the world in their habitats. He formed **3.** _____

about how and why populations change. Lots of evidence supports his ideas, so they are

now called **4.** _____. The theory of descent with

5. _____ says that newer species are related to and descended from

earlier species. The theory of **6.** _____ explains that organisms that

are best suited to their environment are more likely to survive and reproduce.

Directions Tell how each pair of terms is alike. Then tell how they are different.

hypothesis/scientific theory

7. Alike: _____

8. Different: _____

descent with modification/natural selection

9. Alike: _____

10. Different: _____

Vocabulary Review

Directions Match each term with its description.
Write the correct letter on the line.

Column A	Column B
_____ 1. adaptive advantage	**A** separation of a population into two populations as a result of a change in the environment
_____ 2. cast	**B** type of fossil that forms when an imprint of an organism fills with minerals
_____ 3. mold	**C** body part that appears to be useless to an organism but was probably useful to its ancestors
_____ 4. fossil record	**D** time required for half a radioactive mineral to decay
_____ 5. hominid	**E** history of life on earth shown by fossils
_____ 6. mass extinction	**F** body parts that are similar in related organisms
_____ 7. half-life	**G** type of fossil formed when a dead organism leaves an empty space in a rock
_____ 8. vestigial structure	**H** time during which large numbers of species die out
_____ 9. geographic isolation	**I** trait that helps an organism survive in a certain environment
_____10. homologous structures	**J** humans and their humanlike relatives